GENDER SENSITIVITY IN SCHOOLS

DR DHEERAJ MEHROTRA

Contents

PREFACE

Gender sensitisation among children teaches them to rely less on subconscious assumptions and generalisations and more on individual personality traits. As an educator, it is essential to explore equality among all odds. Among different gender biases and discriminations. It is important to start educating the students early before they acquire some beliefs regarding gender differences.

The book, Gender Sensitivity in Schools, reflects on the basics and how to develop Gender Equality as a priority in society. A gender-sensitive school has a culture which is boy and girlfriends, orphan and vulnerable child friendly while promoting equity and equality and gender-responsive environments.

Happy Reading!

www.authordheerajmehrotra.com

I
What & Why of Gender Sensitiviy in Schools?

Gender Equality:

"It is time that men and boys recognise the part they must play in gender equality and join with the voices and actions of the women and girls who are trying to re-shape society in the interests of us all."

- Jimmy Carter.

"Gender equality is the goal that will help abolish poverty and create more equal economies, fairer societies, and happier men, women, and children."

• 2 •

- Graça Machel.

"Equal pay isn't just a women's issue; when women get equal pay, their family incomes rise, and the whole family benefits."

- Mike Honda.

MAKE UP IS
GENDERLESS

As an educator, it is essential to explore equality among all odds. Among different gender biases and discriminations. It is important to start educating the students early before they acquire some beliefs regarding gender differences.

The term Gender Equality is very much required to be made in our public discussions and practice with the new world order. The school curriculum requires it at length. The students should be free to select the subject they are interested in; their gender should not influence their choice. A gender-sensitive school has a culture which is boy and girlfriends, orphan and vulnerable child friendly while promoting equity and equality and gender-responsive environments.

What and Why of Gender Equality?

Well, friends, the term gender equality involves empowering all the students identically. As an educator, our work is to eliminate the negative thinking and beliefs from child's minds for the sake of a promising future. This is the way they shall affect society differently.

The importance of teaching and introducing this subject from the base years of education is a requisite. This can help protect them from biases and will be able to guide others also about this. In our days as students, we recall numerous types of discrimination we experienced in classrooms. Hence, it is essential to create the classroom environment so that STEMS subjects' opportunities can be given to every student according to their interest.

It is hard to discuss ways to bring out gender equality in education, and we work the same through the following strategies.

Be the role model for your students

Don't connect gender with an ability

Interact with students about their dreams.

Terms related to Gender sensitivity in schools relate to the following for a better understanding as educators:

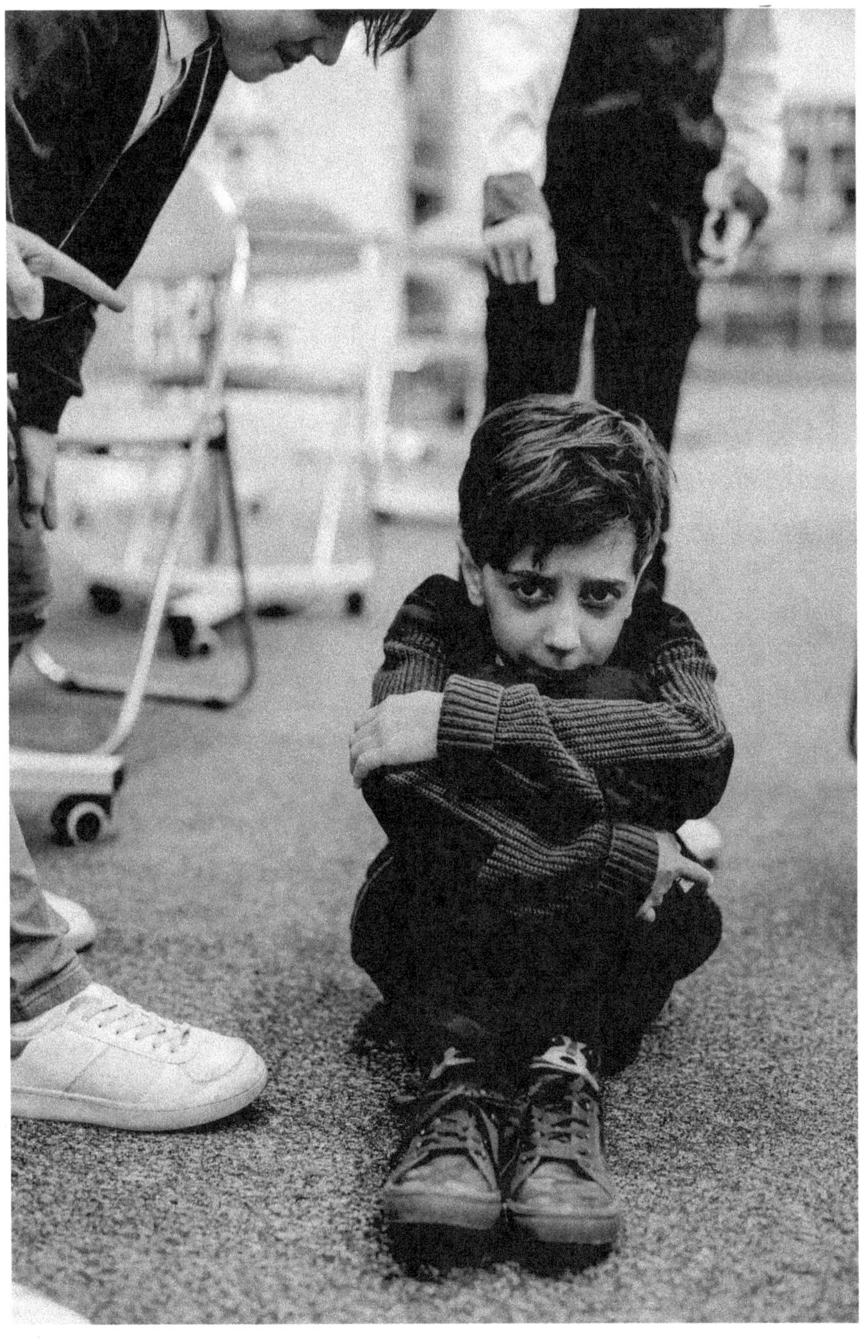

Gender Equality

Well, to define, A "gender-equal society" is a society in which both men and women shall be given equal opportunities to participate voluntarily in activities at all levels as equal partners and shall be able to enjoy political, economic, social and cultural benefits as well as to take responsibilities equally. It exhibits an Equal treatment of women and men in laws and policies and equal access to resources and services within families, communities and the society at large.

Gender Equity

Gender equity is the process of being fair to women and men. To ensure fairness, strategies and measures must often be available to compensate for women's historical and social disadvantages that prevent women and men from otherwise operating on a level playing field. Equity leads to equality. It also reflects fairness and justice in sharing the benefits and responsibilities amongst the masses.

Gender Discrimination

Gender discrimination is when someone is treated unequally or disadvantageously based on their gender but not necessarily in a sexual nature. This includes harassment/ discrimination based on sex, gender identity, or gender expression. Women and girls are most likely to experience the negative impacts of gender discrimination. It can mean restricted access to education, a lower standing in society, less freedom to make decisions around their personal and family life, and lower wages for their jobs and work.

RACISM
IS NOT
OPINION

Socialisation

The role of socialisation is to acquaint individuals with the norms of a given social group or society. It prepares individuals to participate in a group by illustrating the expectations of that group.

Socialisation is the process through which the individual learns to become an accepted member of society.

Socialisation is crucial for children, who begin the process at home with family and continue it at school.

Gender inequality

Gender inequality is discrimination based on sex or gender, causing one sex or gender to be routinely privileged or prioritised over another. Gender equality is a fundamental human right, and that right is violated by gender-based discrimination. Gender inequity has severe and long-lasting consequences for women and other marginalised genders.

Gender inequality affects everyone, including men. Stereotypes or 'rules' about how women and men, girls and boys should begin in childhood and follow us through to adulthood.

Gender Gap

A gender gap, a relative disparity between people of different genders, is reflected in various sectors in many societies. Gender is crucial in defining the power, privilege and possibilities that some people have, and others do not have in a given community. It affects progress towards equality and freedom from discrimination. Differences exist between men and women as reflected in social, political, intellectual, cultural, scientific or economic attainments or attitudes. The gender pay gap results from many factors, including race and ethnicity, disability, access to education and age. As a result, different groups of women experience very different gaps in pay.

Gender Relations

Gender relations define how people should interact with others and how others relate to them, depending on their attributed gender. They should be analysed within the cultural context in which they develop. Good gender relations refer to the mutual respect between men and women or boys and girls. It also refers to giving equal opportunity to both men and women. To build good gender relations, the men and the women or the boys and girls must be given equal opportunities to develop their talents. Gender relations intersect with all other influences on social relations – age, ethnicity, race, religion, etc. – to determine the position and identity of people in a social group. Since gender relations are a social construct, they can be transformed over time to become more equitable.

Gender Roles

Gender roles in society mean how we're expected to act, speak, dress, groom, and conduct ourselves based on our assigned sex. For example, girls and women are generally expected to dress in feminine ways and be polite, accommodating, and nurturing. Gender roles are social constructs that are not based on natural human behaviour. This is because gender roles evolved as a way to organise the necessary tasks done in early human society. Gender roles are cultural and personal. They determine how males and females should think, speak, dress, and interact within the community context.

Gender Stereotype

Gender stereotyping refers to the practice of ascribing specific attributes, characteristics, or roles to an individual woman or man by reason only of her or his membership in the social group of women or men. Myths in education about gender stereotypes might include: boys are slower than girls to read. Girls are naturally quieter than boys. Science and maths are boys' subjects. A gender stereotype is a generalised view or preconception about attributes or characteristics that are or ought to be possessed by women and men or the roles that are or should be performed by men and women. Gender stereotypes can be positive and negative, for example, "women are nurturing" or "women are weak".

Social Construction

Gender is a social construction because it varies across time, place and cultures. Neurology does not determine gender, nor does biology. The social construction of gender is a theory in feminism and sociology about the manifestation of cultural origins, mechanisms, and analogies of gender perception and expression in the context of interpersonal and group social interaction. Social constructivists propose that there is no inherent truth to gender, social expectations, and gender performance construct.

Gender Mainstreaming

Gender mainstreaming is a strategy to improve the quality of public policies, programmes and projects, ensuring a more efficient allocation of resources. Better results mean increased well-being for both women and men and the creation of a more socially just and sustainable society. Gender mainstreaming ensures that policy-making and legislative work is of higher quality and has greater relevance for society because it makes policies respond more effectively to the needs of all citizens – women and men, girls and boys.

Femininity

Femininity (also called womanliness) is a set of attributes, behaviours, and roles generally associated with women and girls. FEMININITY means the quality or nature of the female sex: the quality, state, or degree of being feminine or womanly.

Femininity is authentically growing into power, voice, and strength.

AMANDA GORMAN

Femininity is a double-edged sword. The fact that I get to be feminine in my daily life—with dresses, makeup, heels, and all the rest—is a constant source of joy. But it comes with the inevitable, nagging question: Am I feminine enough?

AMY SCHNEIDER

Patriarchy

Patriarchy is a social system in which men dominate over others, but can also refer to dominance over women specifically; Patriarchy is an analytical concept referring to a method of political, social, and economic relations and institutions structured around the gender inequality of socially defined men and women.

Gender Relationships

Gender relations are how a culture or society defines rights, responsibilities, and the identities of men and women about one (Bravo-Baumann, 2000). Gender relations are shaped by care arrangements in all societies – given women's greater responsibility for care relative to men. Care regimes shape gender regimes and vice versa. Gender relations refer to the social relationships and power distribution between men and women in both the private (personal) and public spheres.

Gender Sensitive School

A gender-sensitive school has a culture which is boy and girlfriends, orphan and vulnerable child friendly while promoting equity and equality and gender-responsive environments.

Suggestions for teachers to promote gender equality within a classroom.

- *Be Reflective and Be Objective*

- *Pay attention to new trends and try giving your students gender-neutral responses about these trends.*

- *Use gender-neutral language*

- *When referring to children, E.g. instead of saying, 'Choose a boy to go with you, say, 'Choose a friend to go with you. Similarly, avoid organising children according to gender, E.g. 'Boys line up here and girls here.' This only reinforces gender segregation.*

-

Avoid stereotyping children

- *E.g. boys are noisy and loud, girls are calm and sweet, boys show less emotion, and girls cry more readily.*

- *Self-regulate your interaction with the children*

- *We tend to comfort girls more and send boys on their way earlier. Encourage all children to share feelings and emotions equally.*

- *Ask all students to participate in a variety of classroom chores.*

- *Seat and Group Students Intentionally*

- *Encourage boys and girls to sit together by making a seating chart.*

- *Use Project-Based Learning*

- *Avoid asking students to speak on behalf of their gender.*

- *Ask students to speak for themselves rather than a larger group. Avoid asking questions with leading intros such as, "How do you think most boys would feel about this story?"*

In addition to the above, the educators must avoid separating supplies or materials by gender. Make sure to Mix costumes and art supplies for younger students rather than dividing them into sections for boys and girls. This will enable students to express themselves creatively without anxiety about adhering to traditional gender roles.

Be a role model as Educators. Children learn by imitation. Behave appropriately with other teachers and students and be coherent with your discourse. Make your behaviour a role model for others to follow. Relevance of Gender in the Competency-Based Curriculum must be a priority for schools.

Ask children to draw their idea. It may be of a firefighter, police officer or nurse. Then invite a female firefighter and police officer, and a male nurse into the classroom. Invite them to discuss their jobs and unpack the children's drawings and expectations about the visitors.

Always use non-gender-specific terms when referring to occupations. Some priorities include Focusing on the meaning and usefulness of gender-responsive school management, which plays a significant role in the achievement of both girls and boys.

Woman visibility is to be in action. Invite women as guest lecturers who can speak about their careers and experience to set an example for students.

Videotape your class to examine your teaching methods. Review to see if you call on students of both genders, listen as intently to girls as you do to boys, and assess what types of questions you ask students of each gender.

Feedback from Colleagues and Students. Get feedback from colleagues on any differences they might notice, and you don't. Try getting feedback from students through an anonymous comment box.

In a Gender Sensitive School:

· Girls are empowered to express themselves freely and confidently within and outside school

· The school community has a good level of awareness of gender issues

· The educators apply gender equality principles in the academic processes

· Girls and boys equally participate in in-door and out-door sports

· School has policy and mechanism to address violence perpetrated by teachers or

students

· *Educators are trained to address and mitigate different forms of violence*

· *The school environment encourages girls to bring out their full academic potential in*

all subjects, particularly in Science and Mathematics

· *The school addresses the issue of needy girls through the provision of scholarships*

· *Dropout rates are lowered*

· *The community is actively involved in the school and in supporting girls to enrol and*

remain in school.

· *Gender Sensitive physical facilities are available-separate toilets, water and sanitation*

· *Guidance and Counseling services are available*

· *Educators have been trained in skills necessary for gender-sensitive teaching*

· *School Management is gender sensitive in approach. In addition, Gendered language use in the classroom and at school is also essential.*

** Gender Responsive Interactions is of need and practice.*

** There is a need for Special Considerations:*

· Focuses on the relevance of the gender-responsive package and elevates the participants' interest and awareness of the gender response pedagogy.

** Emphases the participants to appreciate Gender - Responsive Teaching and Learning Environment and how language can reinforce the existing Gender gaps.*

Reflections & Training Activity for Educators:

Reflect on your school and discuss with your colleagues the questions below:

· Are separate spaces available for boys and girls, inside or outside the classroom?

· When should spaces used by boys and girls be separated?

· Do boys or girls interfere with the others' space?

· Which spaces are neutral, and what characterises them?

· *Who uses the neutral/shared spaces mainly and why?*

· *When there is very little space, who uses it mainly?*

Gendered language use in the classroom and at school Activity 1:

The need to use gender-neutral language in the classroom

· *Gender-neutral language eliminates assumptions about someone's gender identity based on appearance.*

· *It avoids reinforcing gender binaries, and it respects diverse identities.*

· *The use of gender-specific language tends to be biased towards masculine words, contributing to gender power imbalances.*

· *The words children hear affect their perceptions of the gender appropriateness of specific careers, interests, and activities.*

Ask students to discuss in pairs or small groups all or some of the following questions:

• *What would the world be like if gender equality existed everywhere?*

• *What difference do you think it might make to the world?*

• *What difference do you think it might make to you?*

• *Do you feel you can change the world toward gender equality?*

• *Can you think of someone who is a role model for gender equality?*

Gender Neutral

It means not referring to either sex but only to people in general gender-neutral language. This use of 'they' as a gender-neutral pronoun is being revived."

Gendered noun/ gender-neutral noun

man person, individual

humanity people, human beings, humanity

Gender Blindness

Gender blindness describes the practice of ignoring differences between genders, including historical differences in the treatment of various genders. Gender blindness is an ideology where a person chooses not to see differences between genders. Gender blindness can be harmful.

Gender Awareness

Gender awareness is an understanding of socially determined differences between women and men based on learned behaviour—gender awareness raising aims at increasing general sensitivity, experience and knowledge about gender (in)equality.

Gender Sensitiveness or Sensitization

Gender sensitisation refers to the raising sensitisation of gender equality concerns. It helps people examine their attitudes and beliefs and question both sexes' realities. Gender sensitisation refers to the concept of gender sensitivity, recognising gender roles, identifying the privileges and the discrimination existing within genders and creating awareness regarding gender equality. A workplace is a significant place which allows an individual to learn, grow and prosper.

Gender-Based Violence

Using the definition of 'gender-based violence against women from the Explanatory Report to the Istanbul Convention6 as a starting point, we can say that:

Gender-based violence is any harm perpetrated against a person or group because of their actual or perceived sex, gender, sexual orientation and gender identity. Gender-based violence is based on an imbalance of power and is carried out to humiliate and make a person or group of people feel inferior and subordinate. This type of violence is deeply rooted in the social and cultural structures, norms and values that govern society and is often perpetrated by a culture of denial and silence. Gender-based violence can happen in both the private and public spheres, affecting women disproportionately.

According to the UNHCR, Gender-Based violence refers to harmful acts directed at an individual based on gender. It is rooted in gender inequality, power abuse, and harmful norms.

Gender-based violence (GBV) severely violates human rights and is a life-threatening health and protection issue. It is estimated that one in three women will experience sexual or physical violence in their lifetime. During displacement and times of crisis, the threat of GBV significantly increases for women and girls. Quote ref: https://www.unhcr.org/gender-based-violence.html

Gender-based violence is any harm perpetrated against a person or group because of their actual or perceived sex, gender, sexual orientation and gender identity. Studies reveal that Approximately 95% of all victims of violence – whether women or men – experience violence from a male perpetrator.

Gender Empowerment

Gender empowerment is a process by which women can overcome many hurdles, such as education, work status, employment opportunities, health care, social security, and position in decision-making under their gender. For sure, in reality, order, women's empowerment is a critical aspect of achieving gender equality. It includes increasing a woman's sense of self-worth, decision-making power, access to opportunities and resources, power and control over her own life inside and outside the home, and ability to effect change in society.

Gender Sensitive Pedagogy and Teaching Learning Materials

The concept 'gender-sensitive pedagogy' refers to the pedagogical measures deployed to reach gender and equity goals directed differently towards boys and girls as groups. Boys and girls as groups need different approaches to become equal and not restrained by gender.

Gender Sensitive Lesson Planning

Gender can be a sensitive issue for some people, but we believe this lesson gives an engaging fact-finding mission to learn more about the world through the lens of gender equality which is just one of 17 Global Goals.

Teaching and Learning Materials:

The suggested websites include the following:

https://in.pearson.com/blogs/2020/03/how-to-promote-gender-equality-in-the-classroom.html
    https://oceanrep.geomar.de/id/eprint/41854/1/Online%20Material_final_2019.pdf

Teaching Methodologies:

To promote girls and boys equally in coeducational settings, teachers must reflect on their gender stereotypes.

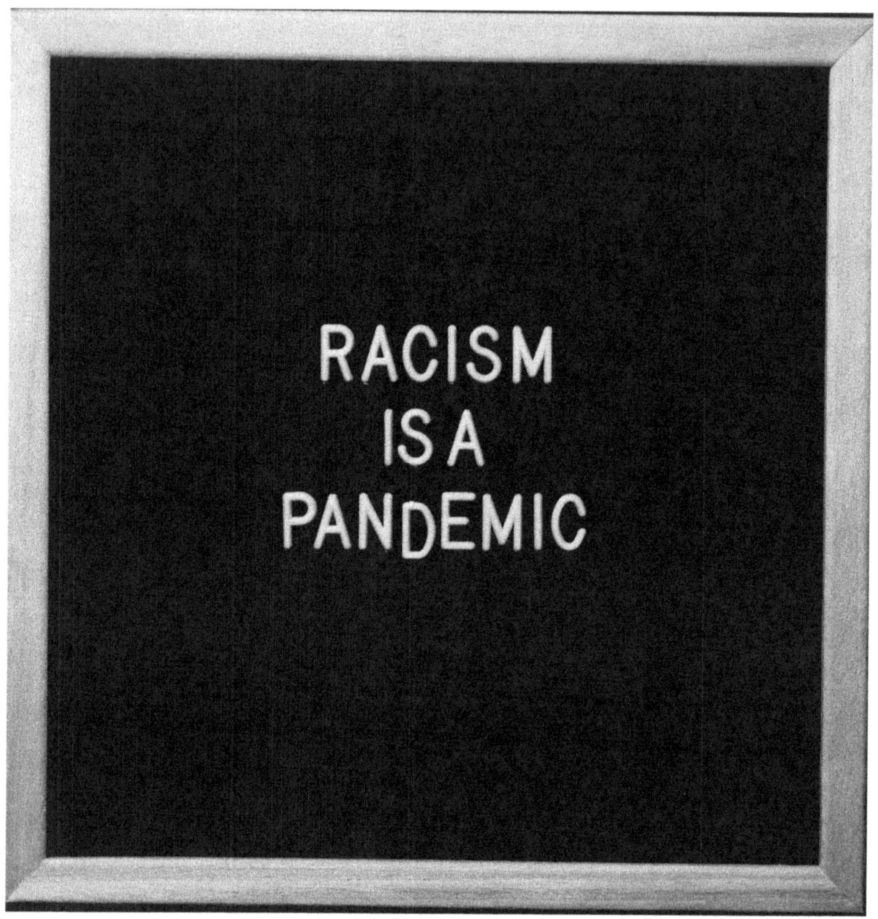

Gender Constraints to Learning:

Constraints that women or men face are a result of their gender. An example of women farmers' constraints might be not having title to their land male-dominated cooperative membership.

Gender Sensitive Sample Lesson Plan

A draft plan for the lesson may go as follows:

Setting up of the Learning Objectives

A Special Mention of :

After this lesson, students will be able to:

Define and explain 'gender equality.'

discuss gender equality in education

hypothesise and research gender equality in their educational community

Length:

1 hour for lesson plus additional time for research and reporting

Materials

Copies of the lesson What Is Gender Equality? - Definition & *Issues, one for each student. Teaching Topics may include the* *following:*

The following Key Vocabulary may be discussed:

1.

   Gender equality

2.

   Equal treatment

3.

   Equal opportunity

4.

   Gender

5.

   Institutional inequality

6.

   Signifiers

℘

girl power

Indicators of gender sensitiveness

While we consider the sensitiveness of the gender issues, the reflections related to the Gender-related Development Index (GDI) adjust the Human Development Index (HDI) for gender inequalities in the three dimensions covered by the HDI: life expectancy, education, and income. Some majorly attributed indicators include the Average hourly earnings of female and male employees by occupation, age and persons with disabilities, Unemployment rate by sex, age and persons with disabilities, Frequency rates of fatal and non-fatal occupational injuries, by sex and migrant status, Labour share of GDP, comprising wages and social protection transfers.

Looking through the 'Gender Lens'- This encapsulates the priority of giving equal status of recognition to each gender.

General Practices for Promoting Gender Sensitivity

Usage of Gender Sensitive Language

Like the one as: Be strong like a boy/ Be strong should be avoided.

• 39 •

Using Gender-Sensitive Language in Classroom: This should be a priority.

Gender-Sensitive Classroom Environment and Interaction: This needs to be put in place.

ॐ

Gender Violence needs to end forever. It is only possible when we treat the genders as equals.

Do's and Don'ts for making Classroom Interaction Gender Sensitive

(Individual Activity)

Following are the few do's and don'ts for making classroom interaction gender-sensitive:

1.

   Do not segregate boys and girls in the classroom in primary classes.

2.

   Appoint two monitors in each classroom, a boy and a girl.

3.

   Make mixed groups for group activities and games.

4.

   Encourage both boys and girls to read aloud, recite and speak on topics related to their immediate lives.

5.

   Make special efforts to direct questions at girls and other shy children.

6.

   Try to 'switch roles' to break down gender barriers and stereotyping of gender roles (which children internalise before reaching school)

7.

Try to relieve girls of domestic chores, orderliness and Cleanliness activities and make both boys and girls share all activities.

8.

Avoid offensive remarks like- 'Are you a girl that you are crying?' or running down the girl who is playful and active as a tomboy.

9.

Prepare girls for leadership and decision-making along with boys.

10.

Plan and conduct activities that allow all children to accept one another as equals.

ॐ

Strategies for integration of Gender Sensitivity in Teaching

The various formats of integration of Gender Sensitivity in Teaching may include engagement as a priority in addition to neutral communication channels.

a. Focus on recent fads and attempt to give impartial reactions about these patterns to your understudies.

b. Even while alluding to kids, E.g. rather than saying, 'Pick a kid to go with you,' say, 'Pick a companion to go with you. Comparably abstain from arranging youngsters as per orientation, E.g. 'Young men line up here and young ladies here.' This just builds up orientation isolation.

c. Try not to generalise youngsters. For example, young men are boisterous, young ladies are quiet and sweet, or young men show less inclination, and young ladies cry all the more promptly.

d. Request that all students take part in an assortment of homeroom tasks.

e. Self-control your association with the kids is a possibility towards equality. Statements like "We will generally comfort young ladies more and send young men on their way prior. " Urge all youngsters to share sentiments and feelings similarly.

f. Emphasise the Seat and Group Students Intentionally. A seating arrangement should Encourage boys and girls to sit together.

g. Organise and implement project-based learning.

h. Get criticism from associates on any distinctions they could notice, and you don't. Take a stab at helping criticism from the students through an unknown remark box or a suggestion box.

છ

These efforts earnestly made in the classrooms by the teachers and heads of schools will enable us to turn the age-old promises of GENDER EQUALITY into action and ensure that we adhere to the plan of sustainable development goals by 2030.

References:

https://in.pearson.com/blogs/2020/03/how-to-promote-gender-equality-in-the- classroom.htmlhttps://in.pearson.com/blogs/2020/03/how-to-promote-gender -equality-in-the-classroom.html

https://www.unhcr.org/gender-based-violence.htmlhttps://www.unhcr.org/gender-based-violence.html

https://www.unicef.org/rwanda/media/1341/file/2017-	National-Gender-Responsive-Teacher-Guide.pdf

https://worldslargestlesson.globalgoals.org/wp-content/uploads/2020/08/ Final-Gender-Equality-Lesson-Plan-1.pdf

https://www.ilo.org/global/topics/dw4sd/themes/equality/ WCMS_560713/lang--en/index.htm

Dheeraj Mehrotra, MS, MPhil, PhD (Education Management) honoris causa., a white and a yellow belt in SIX SIGMA, a Certified NLP Business Diploma holder, is an Educational Innovator, Author, with expertise in Six Sigma In Education, Academic Audits, Neuro-Linguistic Programming (NLP), Total Quality Management In Education, an Experiential Educator, a CBSE Resource towards School Assessment (SQAA), CCE, JIT, Five S, and KAIZEN. He has authored over 100 books on topics which include Computer Science, AI, Digital Body Language, NLP, Quality Circles, School Management, Classroom Effectiveness and Safety and security in schools. A former Principal at De Indian Public School, New Delhi, (INDIA), NPS International School, Guwahati, and Education Officer at GEMS, Gurgaon, with an ample teaching experience of over Two Decades, he is a certified Trainer for Quality Circles/ TQM in Education and QCI Standards for School Accreditation/ School Audits and Management. He has also been honoured with the President of India's National Teacher Award in the year 2006 and the Best Science Teacher State Award (By the Ministry of Science and

Technology, State of UP), Innovation in Education for his inception of Six Sigma In Education by Education Watch, New Delhi and Education World-Best Teacher Award, BOLT Learner Teacher Award by Air India, 'Innovation in Education Award 2016' by Higher Education Forum (HEF), Gujarat Chapter, among others. He has developed over 150 FREE EDUCATIONAL MOBILE Apps for the Google Play Store exclusively for Teachers, Students, and Parents. This work has been recognised by the LIMCA BOOK OF RECORDS & INDIA BOOK OF RECORDS as the only Indian to draw that feast. Dr Mehrotra works as a PRINCIPAL at KUNWARS GLOBAL SCHOOL, Lucknow, in India. He has conducted over 1000 workshops globally on "Excellence In Education" integrated with Total Quality Management and Six Sigma, Technology Integration in Education (TIE), Developing towards being ROCKSTAR TEACHERS, including Cyberspace, Cyber Security, Classroom Management, School Leadership & Management, and Innovative teaching within classrooms via Mind Maps, NLP and Experiential Learning in Academics. He is an active TEDx speaker and can be viewed on the youtube TEDx channel.

As a premium UDEMY Instructor, he has developed over 450 courses and caters to over 8 Lakh students from 180 countries.

He can be visited at www.authordheerajmehrotra.com

BY NATIONAL
AWARDEE
EDUCATOR
Digital List Price: ₹ 72.45
M.R.P.: ₹ 199.00
Kindle Price: ₹ 69.00
Save ₹ 130.00 (65%)
inclusive of all taxes
101
SCHOOL
MANAGEMENT
STRATEGIES
Towards EFFECTIVE
QUALITY MANAGEMENT
System in Schools
DR. DHEERAJ
MEHROTRA
authordheerajmehrotra.com
Flipkart
available at
amazon

FOR
QUALITY
PARENTING
Maximizing
Learning
Potential of Kids
200
WOW PARENTING
SKILLS
DR. DHEERAJ MEHROTRA
amazon
www.authordheerajmehrotra.com
₹269.00
M.R.P.: ₹299.00